Aaron to Zerubbabel

BIBLE MEN IN RHYMES AND QUESTIONS

Rosemary Frantz

Abingdon Press

AARON TO ZERUBBABEL:
Bible Men in Rhymes and Questions

Copyright © 1987 by Abingdon Press

All rights reserved.
No part of this work may be reproduced or transmitted in any form or by any means, electronic or mechanical, including photocopying and recording, or by any information storage or retrieval system, except as may be expressly permitted by the 1976 Copyright Act or in writing from the publisher. Requests for permission should be addressed in writing to Abingdon Press, 201 8th Avenue South, Nashville, TN 37202.

Frantz, Rosemary, 1929–
　Aaron to Zerubbabel.

　Summary: A collection of rhymes about Old and New Testament men arranged in alphabetical order. Each rhyme is accompanied by a question that can be answered by looking up the Scripture reference given.
　1. Bible—Bibliography—Miscellanea—Juvenile literature.
2. Bible games and puzzles—Juvenile literature. [1. Bible—Bibliography—Miscellanea. 2. Bible games and puzzles]
I. Title. II. Title: Bible men in rhymes and questions.

BS572.F73　　　1987　　　220.9'2'088041　　　87-1010
ISBN 0-687-00030-0 (pbk.)

Scripture quotations marked NIV are from the Holy Bible, New International Version. Copyright © 1973, 1978, International Bible Society. Used by permission of Zondervan Bible Publishers.

MANUFACTURED BY THE PARTHENON PRESS AT
NASHVILLE, TENNESSEE, UNITED STATES OF AMERICA

Introduction

Aaron to Zerubbabel is a collection of rhymes about Old and New Testament men, arranged alphabetically. Each rhyme is followed by a question about the man, which can be answered by looking up the Scripture reference given. *Aaron to Zerubbabel* is an educational tool, a learning activity, and an entertaining game!

Designed for use in the home, Christian schools, and Sunday schools, *Aaron to Zerubbabel* encourages children to read the Bible and helps them learn to use Scripture references. Through these rhymes and questions, children, parents, and teachers will meet many fascinating men. In finding answers to the questions, *every book of the Bible* will be used. (Note: For a few letters, only one name or none can be found in either Testament. For letters without proper names, a significant word has been chosen for the rhyme and question.)

A Word to Parents and Teachers

In working through this activity booklet, children will look up seventy-nine separate Scriptures. The spelling of proper names conforms to the New International Version of the Bible, which was used to prepare these rhymes. While any Bible version may be used, the answers to certain questions will be clearer if the NIV is used. Show the children the table of contents in their Bibles, where they can look up the beginning pages of the less familiar books. Talk about the division of each book into chapters and verses, then try some of the rhymes and questions.

You'll soon see many ways this activity booklet can be used. For instance, you can make a game of finding the answers: "Who can find the answer first?" You might also develop reading skills by asking children to read the verse or verses that answer the question. You can go back through the rhymes and questions later, finding out more about the man named by reading some of the verses before and after the reference. Was he a father, a son, a brother? Did he believe in the one God? Was kind of man was he?

After using the activity for a while, make a game of answering the questions without reference to the Scripture verse!

A Word to the Young Reader

The heroes in many of our books seem never to do anything wrong. Our Bible is a very unusual book in that its heroes and heroines are not perfect! Our Lord wants us to know that even when we make a mistake, He still loves us and can use us for His purpose.

In this book, you will meet men who lived in Bible times. Some of the names will seem strange because they are from another language and are not heard in our country. Try saying their names aloud.

To find the answers to the questions about each man, look up the rhyme's Scripture verse in your Bible. Enjoy your search from A to Z!

And the Lord God formed man from the dust of the ground and breathed into his nostrils the breath of life, and man became a living being.

Genesis 2:7 NIV

AARON has two A's in his name,
But that is not his claim to fame.

Who was Aaron's famous brother?
Leviticus 16:1-2

An evil man was king AHAB.
He did things that made God mad.

Whose vineyard did Ahab want?
1 Kings 21:1-2

Paul's letter says:
  "Please aid and equip
friends Zenas and APOLLOS
  for a very long trip."

Who was the lawyer, Zenas or Apollos?
Titus 3:13

BALAAM's donkey would not obey;
The angel of the Lord was in her way.

What three things did Balaam's donkey do?
Numbers 22:23, 25, 27

Paul and BARNABAS went to Jerusalem.
Their good friend Titus went along with them.

Why did Paul and Barnabas go to Jerusalem?
Galatians 2:1-2

BILDAD made three long-winded speeches.
Job was thinking, "He sure preaches, preaches, preaches!"

Who were Job's two other "preachy" friends?
Job 2:11

CALEB walked and walked all over the land.
The land God gave him was very grand.

How old was Caleb when the land was finally given to him? **Joshua 14:10-12**

CLEMENT's name is in the book of life.
He went to heaven, where there is no strife.

Who were the women who worked with Clement?
Philippians 4:2-3

A king of Persia named CYRUS
Put his thoughts upon papyrus.

How many years had Cyrus been king when he wrote these thoughts? **Ezra 1:1**

DANIEL told the king
   what he wanted to know.
God gave him the words
   so long, long ago.

What was the name of the king Daniel talked to?
Daniel 2:25-28

DAVID wrote songs, psalms, and poetry
In praise of his God and his country.

Who were David's father and grandfather? **Ruth 4:17**

DEMETRIUS was very good.
He behaved like all of us should.

Who spoke well of Demetrius? **3 John, verses 11-12**

ELIJAH and ELISHA were prophets
   whose names are almost alike.
They always walked from place to place
   since they didn't have
      a plane or a car or a bike.

How did Elijah go to heaven?
2 Kings 2:11

The gospel taught by EPAPHRAS
Was taught to people of every class.

Who was Epaphras?
Colossians 1:5-7

EZEKIEL spoke mighty words of God.
Even today, some folks think they're odd.

Who was Ezekiel?
Ezekiel 1:1-3

The Bible makes it very clear
   that we should have no FEAR
If a heavenly messenger
   to us should appear.

Who was one person the Lord told not to be afraid?
Genesis 15:1

One man called out to God from what place?
Lamentations 3:55-57

FELIX and FESTUS had
   talked about Paul.
They thought he was mad,
   couldn't understand him at all.

What did Felix want Paul to give to him?

Acts 24:25-26

What did Festus tell King Agrippa?

Acts 25:13-14

The man who advised,
  "Let these men go free,"
Was GAMALIEL,
  the wisest Pharisee.

Did the council follow Gamaliel's advice?
Acts 5:34, 38-40

GEHAZI was very impolite
  to the Shunammite
Who had said, "Everything's all right."

What did Gehazi do to the woman?
2 Kings 4:25-27

The Lord God said to GIDEON:
  "You have too many men,
So I cannot give you
  the camp of Midian."

How many men did God finally let Gideon have?
Judges 7:15-16

You must look, look, and look,
To find the book HABAKKUK.

Which two books of the Bible is Habakkuk between?

HEZEKIAH was one of Judah's best kings.
He broke and smashed all kinds of bad things.

What did Hezekiah break and smash?
2 Kings 18:1-4

There is quite a cost
If you choose to lose
What HYMENAEUS lost.

What did Hymenaeus lose?
1 Timothy 1:18-20

Love is IMMORTAL,
Love never dies.
Love is truthful,
Love never lies.
God is love.

What is going to happen when the last trumpet sounds?

1 Corinthians 15:51-54

ISAIAH told Ahaz of Judah,
"Be careful,
  keep calm,
    and don't be afraid.
The enemies of Judah
  will not invade."

Who were some of the enemies Isaiah named?

Isaiah 7:4-7

Judas ISCARIOT
  betrayed his master, Jesus.
We pray with God's help
  it won't be said of us.

How many silver coins did the priests give Judas?

Matthew 26:14-16

JEHOSHAPHAT, Jehoshaphat,
Was there really a king
With a name like that?

Was Jehoshaphat a good man? **2 Chronicles 20:31-32**

His father was Hilkiah.
He prophesied to King Josiah,
Also to King Zedekiah.
His name was JEREMIAH.

Who promised to protect Jeremiah?
Jeremiah 1:18-19

JOHN ate locusts and wild honey.
He didn't have much use for money.

What kind of clothes did John wear?
Mark 1:6

KADMIEL and all his friends
Told the people,
"Praise the Lord your God,"
And hoped they wouldn't just pretend.

What did Kadmiel and his friends say about God?

Nehemiah 9:5

Let us
Let Jesus
KEEP us.

Where should we keep ourselves?

Jude, verse 21

A fool won't go to school.
He's contrary—
Thinks KNOWLEDGE isn't necessary.

What happened to the people because they lacked knowledge?

Hosea 4:6

LEMUEL wrote Proverbs,
   chapter thirty-one.
He was a faithful,
   obedient son.
He wrote about a wife
   who couldn't be outdone.

Who taught Lemuel his lessons?

Proverbs 31:1

Snoopy barked, "I'm serious."
Lucy crabbed, "It's mysterious."
Charlie Brown sighed, "LINUS, it's miraculous!
A game we've finally won—
   with only one home run!"

Who were the three friends of Linus in the second letter to Timothy?

2 Timothy 4:21

In Sodom lived a man named LOT.
When he left,
It became a hot, hot spot.

What is the name of the other town that became a hot spot too?

Genesis 19:1, 24

The last word in MALACHI's book
   is "curse."
He stopped right there
   so it wouldn't be worse.

What did Malachi say would happen to the fathers and the children?

Malachi 4:6

MELCHIZEDEK was priest forever.
Forever never ends,
Never, never, never.

What did Abraham give Melchizedek?

Hebrews 7:1-2, 17

MOSES led the people out of slavery.
This is true and honest history.

Who were the other two people with Moses?

Micah 6:4

NAHUM's book is number thirty-four.
After it there are only five more.

What city does Nahum talk about?
Nahum 1:1

David did lament,
"NATHAN, I'm not content.
I must repent.
I live in a palace,
While God's ark is in a tent."

What did Nathan tell David to do?
1 Chronicles 17:1-2

NICODEMUS went to
  Jesus one night.
He wanted to learn
  everything right.

How did Jesus answer the question Nicodemus asked?
John 3:4-8

The book of OBADIAH
   has only chapter one.
The book of Obadiah
   has verses twenty-one.

Whose kingdom will be in the mountains, according to Obadiah?
Obadiah, verse 21

OG was a king
Who was tall and fat.
He was a giant—
Just think about that!

How big was Og's bed?
Deuteronomy 3:11

ONESIMUS was sent back home.
He did not want to be in Rome.

Who sent Onesimus home?
Philemon, verses 9-12

First PETER, letter number one.
Second Peter is number two.
These letters tell us we are chosen,
And that is absolutely true.

What are we to do for God, according to First Peter?
1 Peter 2:9

PETHUEL was father of a prophet.
We know about him just this little bit,
And so his name we won't omit.

Who was Pethuel's son?
Joel 1:1

In Egypt PHARAOH was the king.
He did not like Moses' lecturing.

What did the Pharaoh say to Moses?
Exodus 10:28

In the home of Gaius
   there was a meeting.
From our brother QUARTUS
   comes a greeting.

What did Quartus' friend Erastus do?

Romans 16:23

Shh—sh—sh—shh.
At times we must be QUIET
   to hear the Lord God's voice.

What had happened before Elijah heard God?

1 Kings 19:11-12

What should we do when we hear a wise man speak?

Ecclesiastes 9:17

Caesar Augustus
   ordered a census.
Governor QUIRINIUS
   knew he was serious.

Where was Quirinius governor?

Luke 2:1-3

REHOBOAM was the son
of a very wise father.
But as for taking good advice,
he wouldn't even bother.

Who was Rehoboam's father?

2 Chronicles 10:6-8

REUBEN's brother Joseph
was a dreamer.
And his brother Judah
was a schemer.

What happened to Joseph?

Genesis 37:26-30

To help him write
The book of REVELATION,
John was blessed
With an angel's visitation.

Who does the Revelation of John say
will be blessed?

Revelation 1:1-3

When SAMUEL died,
All Israel cried.

Where was Samuel buried?
1 Samuel 25:1

SILAS,* Timothy, and Paul
Wrote words of great encouragement.
Now we can read them all
In the books we call the New Testament.

What do Silas, Timothy, and Paul have that is growing?
2 Thessalonians 1:1-3

*Note: "Silas" is "Silvanus" in some Bible versions.

King SOLOMON
  made a fancy carriage
To take him about
  on the day of his marriage.

What color was the seat in Solomon's carriage?

Song of Solomon 3:9-10

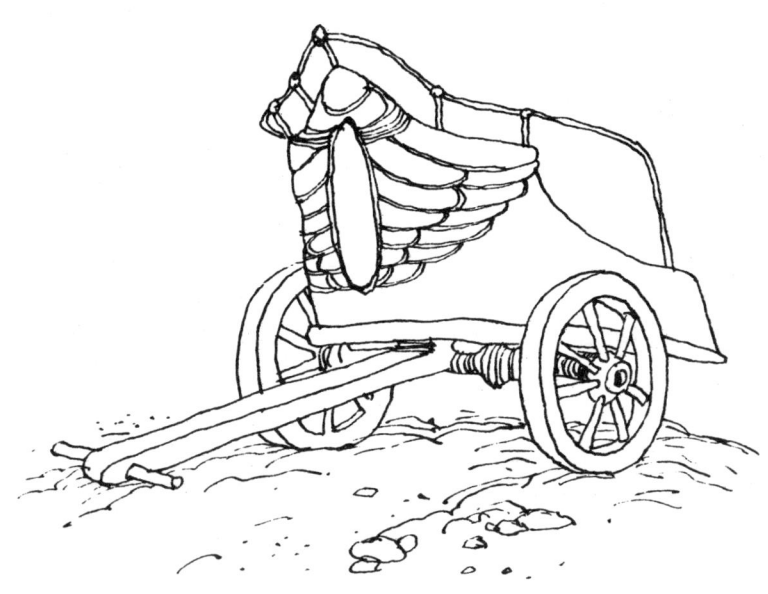

TERAH moved away from home.
For a while he had to roam.

Who was Terah's son?
Genesis 11:31

TIMOTHY was a good news reporter.
That's what he was—
Not a gossip supporter.

What was the good news Timothy gave to Paul from the Thessalonians?

1 Thessalonians 3:6

Paul looked and looked all around town,
But brother TITUS could not be found.

Was Paul upset about Titus?

2 Corinthians 2:12-13

"Yes, I'm serious,"
  fusses old URBANUS,
"Names that end in 'us'
  are much too numerous."

What did Urbanus do?

Romans 16:9

URIAH was strong and brave—a Hittite.
He slept by the palace gate one night.

Who was with Uriah?

2 Samuel 11:9

When UZZIAH was king
The earth did shake.
When Uzziah was king
The earth did quake.

In what country was Uzziah king?

Zechariah 14:5

Only once each can we find these names:
VANIAH,
   Bedeiah,
      and Mattaniah.
They are not in the books by:
Nehemiah,
   Jeremiah,
      or Obadiah.

What had Vaniah and his brothers done?

Ezra 10:35-37, 44

God says, "I guarantee
That faith is the VICTORY."

Who has this victory?

1 John 5:4-5

VOPHSI's son Nahbi
Was sent to scout the land,
To see if the land
Really was grand.

What tribe were Vophsi and Nahbi from?

Numbers 13:14, 16, 30-33

We must decide
  to WALK and follow our guide,
Obey His commands
  and do not hide.

Is the commandment to "walk in love" old or new?

2 John, verses 5-6

WICKEDNESS is really bad.
It makes God fighting mad.

What should you hate?

Psalm 45:7

To what wicked city did God send Jonah?

Jonah 1:1-2

To EXALT means
  to praise and glorify,
To praise,
  to glorify,
    and to magnify.

Who is to be exalted?

Psalm 99:9

The riches of God's grace
  are never commonplace.
His kindness is EXPRESSED to us
  in ways that are continuous.

God's kindness is expressed to us through what person?

Ephesians 2:6-7

King XERXES* ruled lands
  from the west to the east.
He planned a banquet—
  a very splendid feast.
Many people came—
  the greatest to the least.

How many days did King Xerxes' banquet last?

Esther 1:2-5

*Note: "Xerxes" is "Ahasuerus" in some Bible versions.

Elijah prayed
   and the rain did stop.
For several YEARS
   there was not one drop.

How many years was the land without rain?

James 5:17-18

In God's time a day
   could be a thousand YEARS,
Or those thousand years
   could be a day.

Who always keeps promises?

2 Peter 3:8-9

God chose the YOUNG,
Not the old—
Men who were young,
Men who were bold.

Did the Lord raise up prophets or Nazirites from the young men?

Amos 2:11

ZECHARIAH was very old.
When he spoke to Gabriel,
He was much too bold.

What happened to Zechariah?
Luke 1:18-20

ZEPHANIAH has three chapters
In his little book.
It is a book
For which we really have to look.

Who was the king when Zephaniah spoke?
Zephaniah 1:1

ZERUBBABEL, Zerubbabel,
It is a name I like to spell.
Z-E-R-U-B-B-A-B-E-L!

What did the Lord tell Zerubbabel?
Haggai 2:4